Stephen Speight

THE RUNAWAY

Illustrations: Palle Schmidt

Stephen Speight: The Runaway
Teen Readers, Level 1

Series editor: Ulla Malmmose
and Charlotte Bistrup

© 2003 by Stephen Speight and
ASCHEHOUG/ALINEA, Copenhagen
ISBN Denmark 978-87-23-90388-4
www.easyreader.dk

Printed in Denmark by
Sangill Grafisk Produktion, Holme-Olstrup

About the Author

Stephen Speight studied English at Oxford, where he met his future wife. After several years of teaching and lecturing in England, he was invited to take up a post in Dortmund, Germany. Until his retirement in 2001 he taught language, literature, cultural studies and technical English at Dortmund University, and also supervised students on teaching practice. He has published several textbook series and more than twenty stories for language learners. More recently he has edited three course books for senior students on widely-differing topics: newspapers and television, technology, and The Different Faces of Britain. He contributes regular columns to the periodicals Fremdsprachen Frühbeginn ('Diabolical Dialogues') and Praxis des neusprachlichen Unterrichts ('Would you have marked it wrong?'). Extracts from this column have appeared in book form with the title Right or Wrong? He has also published articles on second language conversation, which was the topic of his dissertation. In 1997 he was awarded the University Teaching Prize of Dormund University. Other professional and leisure interests include modern fiction, caravanning, sailing, jogging and playing the harpsichord.

leaflet

Chapter One - At the *cottage*

Meet the Owens. Mother Gaynor, daughter Jane and son Michael. There's another Michael Owen - a *famous* footballer. Michael has one or two problems with his friends *because of* that. He's **not** very good at football! There's no Mr. Owen. Well, there is, but he's got a new 5 wife. He's not *been around* for three or four years. Gaynor is a child psychologist, but she tries not to practise on her children.

They're spending their summer holiday in Denmark this year. Mrs Owen saw a photo of this holiday cottage 10 in a *leaflet,* and liked it a lot. Now she's looking at the leaflet again. It tells them where to find the *key* to the front door. It's under a stone at a corner of the verandah.

They open the front door and go in with some of their *stuff*. 15

"This is nice," Jane says. "It's all wood - floors, walls and *ceilings*." She runs across the living room, down a short corridor, and throws her bag on a bed in a small bed-room.

"This is **my** room," she says. 20

"I bet it's the nicest room," Michael says. "Girls! Oh yes, you've got a nice view down to the water. Mum, Jane's got the nicest room. It isn't fair!"

---

cottage ['kɑtɪdz], a small house
famous ['feɪməs], most people know his or her name
because of [bɪ'kɑz], that's the reason
to be around [ə'raʊnd], to be at home/to be with someone
stuff [stʌf], the things you need to do something, e.g. swimming stuff
key, vignette, page 9
ceiling ['si:lɪŋ], the top of a room

Mrs Own is looking out of the big windows in the living room.

"All the rooms are nice," she says. "And the leaflet says ..." - she has another look at it - "... that there's a second telephone in that bedroom over there. So you can use your laptop in there, Michael."

Michael grins at his sister and puts his bag in the bedroom with the telephone.

"There's no view from in there," his sister says, "but you never look out of the window anyway. You play computer games all the time wherever you are! I don't know why you go on holiday at all."

"Now then!" Gaynor says. "That's no way to start the holiday. It's so lovely here. Let's go and have a picnic down by the water. Michael, you take the coolbox down to the fjord. There are some sandwiches we can eat up, and some cold drinks. Jane, you can look for a *blanket* for us to sit on, and I need to find my sunglasses.

blanket

toe

Michael gets to the water first, and walks up and down a bit. He takes his trainers off and puts a *toe* in the water. It's cold, but not too cold. It's a nice place for a swim - but later. Now he's hungry. He goes back to the picnic box. The others aren't there yet.

"Well, just one sandwich," he thinks. He opens the box. There are no sandwiches in it - just a nearly empty bottle of coke. That's funny.

His sister arrives with a blanket, and sees the empty box.

6

"You've eaten all the sandwiches!" she says.

"No - there weren't any left."

Gaynor arrives in her sunglasses.

"Mum," Jane says, "Michael has eaten all the sandwiches."

Michael hits his sister.

"It's not *true*," he says. "The box was empty. Really,
Mum."

Gaynor looks puzzled.

"That's funny," she says." "I know there were some
sandwiches left - and some cake. Jane, tell your brother
you're sorry. He could never have eaten all that.
Where is our food?"

"Sorry, Michael," Jane says. "Even you couldn't have
eaten all that in a *couple* of minutes. Perhaps they have
wild animals in Denmark ...."

"Oh yes?" Michael says. "What kind of wild animal
can open a coolbox?"

Chapter Two - The missing anorak

In the evening it was a bit cold. They lit a fire in the
iron stove and sat round in the warm. It was lovely and
cosy. But they all felt a bit *uneasy*, and they looked out
of the big windows now and then. Everything was dark
outside, but there was moonlight on the water. It was

---

true [tru:], it's a true story, it really happened
couple ['kʌpl], two or three, or two people who go around together
iron stove, see illustration, page 8
cosy [kouzɪ], warm, safe and comfortable
uneasy [ʌn'i:zɪ], not very happy

iron stove

really very beautiful and very quiet. But they were all thinking…

Gaynor: I'm sure Michael didn't eat all that stuff. So who did? Surely no one *goes hungry* in Denmark - or do they?

5 Michael: I **know** I didn't eat the sandwiches - but

| *to go hungry* [ˈhʌngrɪ], not to have enough to eat

the others think I did! It's just one of those things. I'm going to forget all about it.

Jane: I don't really think Michael ate the sandwiches. You read these stories about animals that *escape* from zoos. Even big cats sometimes. There could be a 5 lion out there - or a wolf. But animals can't open cool-boxes. That's true. So there must be a person out there. Maybe it's a bit too quiet here. I'm going to shut my window this evening, that's *for sure*. I hope I can sleep.

Before they went to bed, all three of them checked 10 that the front door was *locked*. And the back door. Then Gaynor unlocked the front door again and went out to check that the car was locked. Then she came back in and re-locked the front door.

They were tired after the long journey. Soon they 15 were all asleep.

key and lock

Next morning Jane woke early. There was a nice smell in her room - the smell of wood. She sat up and looked out of the window at her view of the long grass, the pine trees and the water. Then she opened her window 20 and took a deep breath. Denmark was really great. The sun was already up. She couldn't wait to have breakfast and get outside. Then she saw something moving -

to escape [ɪˈskeɪp], to run away from a zoo etc.
for sure [ʃɔː], (here) she's really going to do it

something blue. A small figure was moving among the trees, running from one to another, then hiding. Of course - it was Michael, playing one of his games. But she was a bit surprised to see him up so early. That wasn't
5 like him at all.

Then she heard Gaynor's voice from the kitchen.

"Come on, you two. *Rise and shine*. It's a lovely day and we don't want to *waste* it!"

Jane got dressed and went through into the kitchen.
10 A minute or two later Michael came in. He was still in his pyjamas.

Jane smiled.

"You want us to think you've just got up," she said.

"Well, I **have** just got up," Michael said. "Look -
15 pyjamas."

"But I saw you out there in the pines, about ten minutes ago. I know it was you because you were wearing your old blue anorak. I'd know it anywhere."

"But I **wasn't** out there. Why would I get up early
20 when I'm on holiday?"

"Good question," said Gaynor. "Now let's get on with our breakfast, shall we."

"But there's a puzzle here," Jane said. "I'm sure that was Michael's anorak."

25 Michael suddenly looked a bit worried.

"I think I left my anorak out on the verandah last night," he said, and ran out of the kitchen.

He was soon back again.

"It's gone," he said.

---

rise and shine [rɑɪz] [ʃɑɪn:], get up and look happy
to waste [weɪst], turn off the lights - we don't want to waste electricity

10

"Well," Gaynor said, "I didn't think there was much crime in Denmark, but I'm beginning to think again. First the sandwiches, and now Michael's anorak. We'll just have to be very careful. We mustn't leave things lying around. Perhaps there's a very *naughty* little boy in 5 one of the other cottages. We're not going to let him - or anyone else - *spoil* our holiday. Now, what shall we do today? Anyone want to go for a swim?"

"Not yet, Mum," Michael said. "It's pretty *chilly* out there. We could go swimming this afternoon." 10

"Jane, what would you like to do?" Gaynor asked.

"I'd like to go to the next town, wherever that is," Jane said.

"Well, we did come here to get away from towns," Gaynor said, "but we need to buy some food for the 15 next few days. Why not. Michael, what do you think?"

"Can I have a new anorak? The blue one was very old anyway."

"Hmm. I think things are a bit expensive in Denmark - but they aren't exactly cheap in Wales, either. 20 OK, then, we'll look for a new anorak for you. But I'm not *paying the earth* for a famous *brand name*."

"I'm not coming, then. I can have a look round here - or go back to bed for an hour or two."

"If we leave you here, you'll only play computer 25 games. I'm sure we can find something you like at a *sensible* price. We'll clear up while you go and get dressed

naughty ['nɔːti], a child who isn't being good is naughty
to spoil [spɔil], to take the fun out of something
chilly ['tʃili], a bit cold
to pay the earth [pei] [ɜːθ], to pay a lot too much money for something
brand name ['brænd neim], Nike, Coke and Mercedes are famous brand names
sensible ['sensəbl], (here) not too expensive

11

- but tomorrow it's *your turn* in the kitchen."

As they went out to the car, Michael ran round to the side of the verandah. The ground was sandy, but he could see that there were *footprints*.

footprints

Danish pastry

5   "Someone was here all right," he called.

They drove off to Thisted, looking back over their shoulders a couple of times on their way to the main road.

Michael got a new anorak in Thisted. It was red - a 10 very Danish colour. Jane bought a CD, and Gaynor bought some food in a supermarket called Super-Brugsen. They had coffee and *Danish pastries* in a nice little café.

When they got back to the cottage, Michael's blue 15 anorak was hanging over the verandah railing.

"Well!" Michael said. "What do you think of that?"

"You don't need a new anorak now," Jane said. "We can take it back to the shop. We've got the bill, and it's still got the *labels* on it."

20   "That's not fair!" Michael said. "I **like** my new anorak, and I'm keeping it."

your turn [tɜːn], next time it's your job
labels ['leibl], (here) the little tickets on new clothes

12

"Quite right, Michael," Gaynor said. "We're not taking it back. You can *keep it for best*, and wear the old one around the cottage. I hope you won't need it anyway."

"I've been thinking," Jane said. "If you ask me, this 5 boy isn't here with his family, he isn't naughty, and he isn't a *thief*. He just *borrowed* Michael's anorak because he was cold in the night. And he took our food because he was hungry and he hasn't got any money."

"Or he couldn't get to a shop to buy anything to eat," 10 Gaynor said. "The nearest shop is *several* miles away."

"If he's run away from home, he won't want people to see him," Jane said. "If he went into a shop someone could *recognize* him."

"Only if he lives round here," Michael said. "If he's 15 run away, he'll have tried to get as far from home as possible."

"Hey, *hang on* a minute," their mother said. "I think you two have been watching too much television!"

"But the sandwiches went," Jane said. 20

"And someone - a boy about my size - took my anorak and put it back again," Michael said. "So I don't think we're *making it all up*."

"Well," their mother said, "Perhaps you're right. If it is a boy who's run away from home, he must be very 25 unhappy, and he may need help. Let's see if we can make contact with him."

---

to keep something for best, only to wear it on special days
thief [θi:f], someone who takes other people's things (steals things)
to borrow ['bɒrəʊ], to take something which you want to give back later
several ['sevrəl], more than a few
to recognize ['rekəgnaɪz], to see someone and know who it is
hang on ['hæŋ ɒn], - wait (a minute or a second)
to make something up, to 'tell stories' that aren't true

13

Chapter Three
One *trap* - and two boat trips

On their next shopping trip they bought two Danish apple cakes, one for them, and one for the runaway. They ate the first cake, of course, and they left the second cake on the verandah table.

5   "We can't leave the table in the middle of the veran-dah," Jane said. "No one would *risk* taking it from there. Let's move the table to the side - near where Michael left his anorak."

So they moved the table, and they put the cake at
10 the side of the table, near the *railing*. Then they went inside, and *took it in turns* to watch the verandah. Two hours later the cake was still there.

railing

string

frying pan

It's a bit boring, watching a cake on a table.

"It's getting damp out there," Gaynor said. She went
15 out and put a plastic bag over the cake. She looked around, but she couldn't see or hear anything except the soft sound of the water on the beach and the wind in the long grass.

It was getting late, time for the children to go to bed.

to risk [rɪsk], firemen sometimes have to risk their lives
to take it in turns, first one person does something, then a second per-son does it

"If I was out there, I'd just have to get that cake somehow," Michael said. "It looks very *inviting*."

"Perhaps he's just not there any more," Jane said. "I'm tired of looking at a cake all evening. Even television you can't understand is more interesting. I'm going to bed." 5

"I'm tired, too - and I'm not going to sit here all night," Gaynor said. "What do we do now?"

"We could *fix* a piece of *string* to the cake and tie it to a *frying pan* on the kitchen table," Michael said. 10 "Then, when he takes the cake, the pan will fall down, and we'll all wake up. I read about the idea in a comic."

Nobody could think of a better idea, so they fixed up Michael's trap, and then they all went to bed.

inviting [ɪnˈvaɪtɪŋ], (here) just asking someone to take it
to fix [fɪks], (something up) to put something ready

15

About an hour later there was a loud crash. All three of them woke up. Their hearts were *thumping*. They ran to the verandah, and of course the cake was gone - and so was the runaway.

to thump

Thump!
Thump!
Thump!

5   Next morning at breakfast on the verandah they tried to decide what to do next.

"Let's just forget about him," Jane said. "If we don't, this silly business is going to spoil our holiday."

"I think you're right, Jane" Gaynor said. "After all, 10 he's not *dangerous*. Let's just carry on as normal. We can leave some food out now and then - we know he gets hungry, don't we!"

"I think we should set another trap," Michael said. "A better one this time."

cover

elephant trap

dangerous ['deindʒərəs], a crocodile is a dangerous animal

16

"How about an *elephant trap?*" his sister asked. "I expect you've read about them in one of your comics, too. You know, you dig a big hole in the ground, with a *cover* over it so the elephant doesn't see it. You'd have to leave out the *spikes*, of course." 5

"Ha ha, very funny," Michael said.

"Let's not talk about him any more," Gaynor said. "What shall we do today? Any bright ideas?"

"I'd like to pump up the *inflatable* and go out on the fjord," Michael said. "You did say I could use the *out-* 10 *board* this year, Mum. I'm really *looking forward* to it. It's the main reason I'm here!"

"Well, OK. Jane, do you want to go out with him? You can keep an eye on your brother for me. I'm just going to sit here on the verandah in the sun." 15

"I don't really want to go out with Michael," Jane said. "I always get *a wet bottom* in the boat."

"Come on, Jane," her brother said. "I won't go very fast - promise - and then you won't get wet. We could cross to that little island. That would be exciting." 20

"Much **too** exciting," Gaynor said. "That island is miles away. Anything could happen. You can just *cruise around* where I can see you - and don't forget your *life- jackets.*"

"Mum, please ..." 25

"Sorry, Michael. That's what mums are for - to stop children taking too many risks."

spikes

inflatable [ɪnˈfleɪtəbl], *outboard* [ˈaʊtbɔːd], *see illustration page 18*
to look forward to [lʊk ˈfɔːwəd], *to want something nice to happen*
a wet bottom [ˈwet ˈbɒtəm], *when you sit in water you get at wet bottom*
to cruise around [kruːz], *to 'drive' around on a boat*
lifejackets [ˈlaɪfjækɪt], *see illustration, page 18*

lifejacket

inflatable

outboard

It wasn't very easy to start the outboard, but it went in the end, and the two children spent a happy morning out on the water.

"What I'd like is a jet-ski" Michael said. "Two *horse-*
5 *power* just aren't enough. Jet-skis are really fast."

"And really noisy," Jane said. "I think they're horrible. What I'd like is a nice sailing boat - like that one over there. You don't have to be a millionaire..."

They used up all the petrol in the outboard and had
10 to paddle back.

In the afternoon all three of them went out in the car to fill up the petrol *canister* for the outboard and do a bit of shopping.

horsepower ['hɔːspaʊə], this car has a 250 horsepower engine. Wow!
canister ['kænɪstə], see vignette, page 19

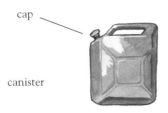

cap

canister

When they got back, Michael ran down to the water with the canister of petrol. He took the *cap* off the little petrol tank and found that it was half full. And the engine was hot.

"Someone has been out in the boat while we were away," he thought. "Our runaway has been in action again. I wonder what he needed the boat for - and where he got the petrol from." He looked around inside the boat but he didn't find anything. Then he looked at the sand round the boat, and found a small card.

He knew what it was - a *scratch-card* for a mobile phone.

"That's why he needed the boat," Michael thought. "He must have gone across to *a garage* on the island. You can get cards at places like that. Lucky him! We had to stay here in the bay. I wonder who he needed to call. I hope he's OK. I don't know him, but he's beginning to seem like a friend".

He went back and told the others what he had found. That evening a woman from one of the other holiday cottages came to the door. First she spoke Danish, and Gaynor explained that they didn't understand. Then she spoke English - very good English, too.

scratch-card [skrætʃ], a little card with a hidden number on it. You scratch the card (an angry cat scratches) to find the number
garage ['gærɪdʒ], place where you can buy petrol, diesel - and usually other things, too

scratch-card

"*Sorry to bother you*," she said. "I was sure there was still some petrol in my car - but when I tried to start it just now, it was empty. I can't understand it. *I suppose you couldn't* lend me some - just enough to get to a
5 garage. I'm a doctor. I'm on holiday here, but sometimes I get an *emergency call*, and then I need the car - fast."

"No problem," Michael said. "We bought some petrol for our outboard today, and we didn't need most
10 of it. It's still in the canister. I'll run down and get it for you."

sorry to bother you ['bɒðə], I hope it's not a problem
I suppose [sʌ'pəʊz] you couldn't..., perhaps you could...
emergency call [ɪ'mɜ:dʒənsɪ] , if there's a bad accident, someone has to
make an emergency call to a doctor

"Thanks - that's very kind of you."

"Well, not really," Michael said. "You see, I think the petrol from your car ended up in our outboard motor."

"What? I don't understand."

But **you** understand, don't you. And when Michael explained, the Danish doctor understood, too.

Chapter Four - With the runaway

The runaway only just had time to hide before the Owens got back. She - yes, she's a girl called Anna - watched Michael as he went down to the boat, checked the petrol and found her card.

"I'm leaving *clues*," she thought - in Danish, of course. "A good job he didn't look for footsteps in the sand. He'd have come straight to these bushes."

Why did Anna run away from home, and why did she need a phone card so badly?

It's quite a long story.

She comes from a one-parent family, just like Jane and Michael. Well, it was a one-parent family after her father died, but a year ago her mother married again, and now there's a new baby in the house. Anna doesn't like her *stepfather* very much - she was happier with just her mum, Kirsten, around the house. Lars, her stepfather, is a very big man. He seems to fill the house and not leave room for her. And he leaves his stuff everywhere - *shaving stuff* in the bathroom, magazines on the

clue [kluː], something that helps a detective to catch a thief
stepfather ['stepfɑːðə], you have a stepfather if your mother marries a man who isn't your real father
shaving stuff, see vignette, page 22

curtains

shaving stuff

sofa, dirty plates and coffee cups in the kitchen. And he tries so hard to be friendly. That just makes it worse. She'd like him to stay as far away from her as possible.

After a few months Anna was beginning - just begin-
5 ning - to think it wasn't so terrible after all to have a dad again. When her bike lost a *pedal*, Lars repaired it. They had nice meals out - something her mother couldn't *afford* before Lars joined the family. He bought her one or two little presents - really nice things, too.

10 But then her mother became *pregnant*. From that moment on, the new baby became the centre of every-thing - **everything**! And it wasn't even there yet. No more little presents for Anna - little (and big) things for the baby instead. Its room was painted, a little bed
15 arrived, baby clothes, pretty *curtains*... It made Anna sick. Both her mother and her stepfather told her she

flat tyre

pedal

afford [ə'fɔːd], to have enough money to buy something
pregnant ['pregnənt], with a baby on the way (expecting a baby)

22

was still very important, but she didn't *believe* them. From now on the new baby was number one in the house, and she was *playing second fiddle*. Most of the time they didn't seem to notice she was there.

Then the baby arrived - in the middle of the night, of course. Anna was alone at home, and Lars was with Anna's mother in the hospital.

He rang her early next morning.

"Come and see the new baby! You'll love him! Kirsten is fine. We're so happy."

Anna had her breakfast first. After all, the baby wasn't going to run away. One or two *tears* fell into her muesli. Then she had a happier thought - no school this morning! She rang the school and *explained* about the new baby. Of course they said she could go and see it. Why did everyone seem to think a new baby was good news?

She got out her bike and rode to the small local hospital. There were big *signs* everywhere, so she soon found the right room. There was her mother holding the baby, and Lars with a silly grin on his face. There was a *huge* vase of flowers on the little table. Anna didn't know what to say.

"Look, darling. Your little brother. Isn't he sweet!"

The baby was very small, very red, very *wrinkled*,

---

to believe something [bɪliːv], to think something is true
to play second fiddle [fˈɪdl], to be less important than another person
tears [tɪə], water from your eyes
to explain [ɪkˈspleɪn], to tell someone all about something so that they understand it
sign [sɑɪn], road signs tell you which way to go, when to stop etc.
huge [hjuːdʒ], very big
wrinkled [ˈrɪnkld], with little lines all over it

and it didn't have any hair.

"Sweet???" she thought.

"You can hold him for a minute if you're very care-ful."

5   Kirsten held the baby out towards Anna.

"You have to put a hand under his little head - he can't hold it up yet."

Her mother more or less pushed the sleeping baby into Anna's arms. It seemed to weigh next to nothing.

10 And that was what she felt when she looked at it - nothing.

body

She just stood there like a *statue* holding the baby. It opened its eyes and looked at her, then it began to cry. First quietly, and then louder and louder. The *howls* from that tiny *body* filled the whole hospital.

This was just too much for Anna. She pushed the baby back into her mother's arms, then she turned and ran out of the room, down the corridor, out of the hospital. She jumped on her bike and rode away. Away from the hospital, from school, from home, away from Kirsten and Lars, and away from the horrible baby.

All she had with her were the clothes she was wearing, her *purse* and her mobile phone. She never went anywhere without it. After about ten miles she stopped and sat down at the side of the road. What next? She looked in her purse. She had a fifty Kroner note and a few coins. It was early summer, but the nights were still cold. Where could she sleep? Where would it be safe in the daytime?

purse

Once, while her father was still alive, they had spent a very happy summer in a holiday cottage on the other side of the fjord. There were a lot of holiday cottages there, and plenty of trees and bushes. Some of the cottages would be empty. No one would find her there.

She had enough money for the ferry - and it left from

---

statue ['stætʃuː], a 'picture' made of stone
howl [haʊl], some dogs howl at the moon

a place just down the road. When she got there, the ferry was ready to leave. She pushed her bike on board and sat down on one of the benches.

A man came round to collect the ticket money. "No school today, then?" he asked.

"Er - no. Not for me," she said. And it was true, wasn't it.

She watched the water rushing past the ferry and thought, "I'm running away and I'm not going back." She began to feel free - and happy. Happy for the first time in months.

She spent the first night in a kind of *shed* which was part of one of the holiday cottages.

She watched for a while first to make sure the cottage was empty, then she tried the door of the shed. It wasn't locked. She went in, and pulled her bike in after her.

By now it was quite late, but it wasn't very dark. She left the door a bit open and had a look around. The owners of the house kept their gardening tools and garden furniture in there. There were even some big *sun lounger cushions* for her to lie on. There wasn't room to open out one of the loungers, so she slept on the cushions on the floor. It was quite comfortable, but very cold without any *bedding*.

The next night she was very pleased to find an anorak on the verandah railing of one of the other cottages. The night after that was much warmer, so she gave it back. And then the people in the cottage had very kindly put out a cake for her. Something was hold-

---

bedding ['bediŋ], blankets etc.

shed

sun lounger

cushion

ing it, so she had to pull at it - there was a very loud crash from the cottage. She ran for her life, and just got back inside the shed before lights went on in the cottage.

A few days later the fun was over. Her clothes were 5 dirty, most of her money was gone, and when the cake was gone, she had nothing to eat. She had no *bank account*, and there wasn't a bank for miles *anyway*. To make things worse her stupid bike had a *flat tyre*. Her pump was at home - and so was her *repair kit*.

It was time to get in touch with her best friend, 5 Louise.

She got out her mobile phone and turned it on. Good! The battery was still OK. She pressed the button for Louise's number ..... and a message *appeared* to tell her that she needed a new card.

10 You know what happened next, don't you.

Chapter Five
Friends together, friends *apart*

Anna gave her friend Louise a list of things she needed. Money and food, a repair kit for her bike, some clean clothes. Louise came over on the ferry with all the things in a bag on the back of her bike. She told her 15 parents she was going for a long bike ride, which was true, more or less. They told her to be careful, but they weren't really *worried*. Denmark is a *pretty* safe country.

---

bank account ['bæŋkəkaʊnt], most people keep their money in a bank account - you can put money into an account, take it out when you need it, and your pay goes into it every month
flat tyre ['flæt 'taɪə], see vignette, page 22
anyway ['enɪweɪ], - Oh, I've broken your sun lounger. - Don't worry - it's a very old one anyway
repair kit [rɪ'pɛə 'kɪt], a box with things you need to repair a flat tyre
to appear [ə'pɪə], if something appears you can see it now, but you couldn't see it earlier
apart [ə'pɑːt], not together
worried ['wʌrid], not happy about something
pretty ['prɪti], (here) pretty safe is a bit less than very safe

28

How did the girls meet up? Well, Anna asked Louise to wait at a small crossroads near the holiday cottages. Louise got there just before eleven. That was when they wanted to meet. She stopped and looked around. No sign of Anna. She sat down at the side of the road and waited - and waited. Two or three cars went past. Half an hour is a long time when you're waiting for someone.

Louise felt a hand on her shoulder and nearly jumped out of her *skin*.

"Hi," Anna said (in Danish). "I'm so happy to see you - and thanks for coming."

"You're late!"

"I know. People arrived at the cottage where I'm staying - in the shed, that is. I had to wait for them to take all their stuff inside before I could get away."

The girls went back in among the trees. Anna didn't want anyone to see her.

"Everyone is looking for you," Louise said. The police, too. Your picture has been in the newspaper."

"I'm lucky then. I haven't seen any police round here. I'm not that hard to find!"

"There's been a bank robbery in Thisted. I suppose they've been too busy to look for you."

The girls sat down under the trees and had something to eat and drink. Anna was very hungry.

"Come home with me," Louise said. "We can get your bike from the shed and repair your tyre. You can't live like this for ever!"

"I know. But I can't go back. I just **can't**. It's not my home any more with that new baby there."

skin [skɪn], when it's sunny, you need to put some sun cream on your skin

"That's silly, Anna. Your parents are *desperate*. You're not being fair to them."

"Maybe not. But they're not being fair to me. And only Mum is a real parent anyway. I'm staying here."

Mid-afternoon Louise had to set off for home. Her parents would be worried - and *suspicious* - if she got back late. The girls gave each other a big hug and said goodbye.

Anna watched her friend ride off down the road, then she had a good *cry*. But she wasn't going back. She was happier on her own.

But there was a new problem now. Now that there were people in 'her' cottage, her comfortable life in the shed was over. She needed somewhere else to spend the night. When it got dark she went round looking for an empty cottage. She found one, but everything was locked up. The verandah was nearly a metre above the ground. She could sleep under it - no problem. The weather was still fine - so fine that she hadn't asked Louise to bring an anorak. She put the bag with the things from Louise in it under the verandah, and went back to the shed to get one of the big cushions. Oh no! There was a new *padlock* on the door. Well, it didn't really matter. She could use the bag as a pillow, and the ground was soft and sandy. She could think of a way to get her bike back later.

padlock

desperate ['despərət], very worried, not knowing what to do next
suspicious [sə'spɪʃəs], thinking that something is wrong
a cry/to cry [kraɪ], when tears come from your eyes

gap

plank

drips
of rain

In the evening she *lay* down under the verandah. It was nice there, nicer than in the shed. She did wonder a bit about *snakes* and *spiders*, but she only saw a small field mouse. It was more frightened than she was. When it got dark, she looked up at the stars through the *gaps* between the *planks*. She was soon asleep. 5

Denmark isn't like the *Mediterranean*. Sometimes the weather is beautiful, and sometimes it isn't. So far Anna - and the Owens - had been very lucky. But a *change* was on the way. 10

snake

spider

to lie [laɪ], *lay* [leɪ], *lain* [leɪn], you lie down when you go to bed
Mediterranean [medɪtəˈreɪnɪən], Italy, Turkey and Morocco are all on the Mediterranean Sea
a change [tʃeɪndʒ] (in the weather), from sun to rain - or rain to sun

During the night the stars *disappeared* one by one. At about three in the morning it began to rain. An hour later Anna woke up. She was very wet and very cold. Water was *dripping* through the gaps between the
5 planks. And it was dripping straight into the bag and onto her clean clothes. It rained all day. Anna *slipped* out a couple of times to go to the toilet under the trees, but the rest of the time she was just stuck under the verandah, getting wetter and wetter.

10 The next night she had *trouble* getting to sleep. She was *sneezing*, and her arms and legs felt stiff. In the morning she didn't want to move. She didn't feel like eating. The bread and biscuits Louise had brought were wet anyway. She lay down again.

15 "I must be ill," she thought. "What am I going to do?"

Chapter Six - The body on the steps

The next morning it was still raining. The Owens got up late and took their time over breakfast. Nobody really knew how to spend the day. They *decided* to go shopping in the afternoon if it *cleared up* - or if it didn't.
20 And there was still half the morning to fill. Michael wanted to go back to bed, but Gaynor wouldn't let him.

---

to *disappear* [dɪsə'pɪə], if something disappears, you can't see it any more
to *drip/dripping* [drɪp], see illustration, page 31
to *slip* [slɪp] (out), (here) to move out quickly and quietly, trying not to be seen
trouble, ['trʌbl], problems
to *sneeze* [sni:z], when English people sneeze, they say "Atishoo!"
to *decide* [dɪ'saɪd], they could lie in the sun or go swimming - they decided to go swimming
to *clear up* ['klɪə'ʌp], when the rain stops and the sun comes out

He went into his room anyway and turned on his computer. Jane put a disc in her walkman and started to write postcards. Gaynor wanted to ask them to help with the washing up, but she decided not to. She really didn't mind doing it herself for once - the children usually helped, after all. Well, they helped sometimes - now and then.

It was very quiet in the cottage. You could hear a beep now and then from Michael's computer. Dee-di-di-dee-di-di-dee came from Jane's earphones, and there were small clinking sounds from Gaynor at the *kitchen sink.*

kitchen sink

But then there was another sound. Jane couldn't hear it, of course. Michael didn't hear it because he was miles away, trying to break into a *secret room* on his computer. Gaynor was the one who heard it. It was a kind of *groan.*

She called to the children.

"Is one of you making funny noises?" No answer. She went into Michael's room - no sound. Then she went and *tapped* Jane on the shoulder. "Did you make a funny noise just now?"

Jane took off her earphones. "Did you say something, Mum?"

---

secret room ['si:krət], a room you can't find or can't get into
groan [grəʊn], the noise you make when you are ill or sad
to tap [tæp], to hit (but not very hard) with your fingers or a stick etc.

"Yes. I asked if you made a funny noise."

"No. What kind of noise?"

"Well, it sounded like a kind of groan. Listen - there it is again."

5 "It is a groan - it's coming from outside," Jane said.

They opened the front door and looked out. At first they couldn't see anything, but then they heard the groan again and took two or three steps forward. There was something - or someone at the bottom of the
10 verandah steps.

Jane ran down the steps. Now she could see that it was a girl.

"Hey," she said. "Are you OK? We heard a groan."

Anna - it was her, of course - opened her eyes.

"I think I'm ill, " she said. "Everything hurts and I can't *breathe* very well." 5

They helped Anna to get up, then took her into the house and onto a sofa in the living room. She lay down and closed her eyes again.

"Run across to the doctor's cottage and ask her to come," Gaynor said. "I'll make a hot drink for this young lady - she's wet through and very cold. I don't think a hot drink can do her any *harm*." 10

A few minutes later Jane was back with the doctor. She examined Anna quickly, then she stood up. 15

"She's got *flu*," she said. "It's pretty bad, and it could turn into *pneumonia*. She needs some antibiotics. There's a *chemist's* in town ..."

"I'll go right now," Gaynor said. "Could you write the *prescription* for me, please." 20

"Of course." The doctor pulled a pad out of her bag and *scribbled* a few words on it.

"That should *do the trick*," she said.

The kettle started to whistle in the kitchen.

---

to breathe [briːð], to 'pump' air in and out of your body (your lungs)
(*to do someone*) *harm* [hɑːm], to hurt them in some way
flu [fluː], short for influenza - like a cold but worse
pneumonia [njuːˈməʊnɪə], much worse than flu - it attacks your lungs
chemist's [ˈkemɪst], the shop where you can get medicine, tablets etc.
prescription [prɪˈskrɪpʃn], the piece of paper the doctor gives you to take to the chemist's
to scribble [ˈskrɪbl], to write very quickly
to do the trick [trɪk], to put something right, (here) to make Anna feel better

"Oh," Jane said. "Mum wanted to make a hot drink for the girl."

"A very good idea," the doctor said. "Some kind of tea will be fine - with some sugar in it."

5 "Would you like a cup, too?" Jane asked.

"Yes please, but no sugar for me."

Jane came back with the two cups of tea. She gave the doctor her cup, then went over to the girl on the sofa."

10 "Here," she said. "I've made you a nice cup of tea. Try to sit up and drink it."

She took Anna's arm and helped her to sit up. Anna *sipped* her tea.

"Well, young lady," the doctor said. "Would you like 15 to tell us your name?"

"Anna," said Anna.

"And you have a second name, too, I suppose."

"I don't want to tell you," Anna said.

"Why not? ...... Just a minute ....," the doctor went 20 over to Anna and pushed her dirty hair out of her face. "I've seen your photo in the paper. You've run away from home, over in the Aalborg area. Your name is Anna Hansen, Jensen, something like that."

Anna started to cry.

25 All this time Michael was trying to get into the secret room in his computer. He heard Anna crying and came into the living room.

"What's going on? Who's this, and why is the doctor here? Where's Mum?"

30 The doctor smiled.

| *to sip* [sɪp], to drink slowly, a bit at a time

"You're missing all the *excitement*. This is Anna the runaway. But she isn't running anywhere at the moment. She's got flu - quite badly. She's been *sleeping rough* for the last couple of nights."

Now Michael was excited. 5

"Of course! This is the girl who borrowed my anorak, took our cake and stole some petrol from your car for our outboard. Only we thought it was a boy."

"That's rather sexist of you," the doctor said. "Girls can be runaways, too." 10

Gaynor arrived with the medicine. Anna washed down some tablets with the rest of her tea, then lay down again.

They put a blanket round her and she was soon asleep. 15

"Well," Gaynor said. "We'll have to phone her parents. They must be very worried."

"Yes, they are," the doctor said. I read about it in the newspaper. They've been looking everywhere for her - but not here among the holiday cottages. It's a good 20 place to hide."

"Did it say why she ran away?" Jane asked.

"No. It did say that there's a new baby in the family."

"I can't really remember what it was like when Michael was born," Jane said. "I don't think I was too 25 happy about it, though."

"No, you weren't. You made a terrible *fuss*. You wanted all the *attention* for yourself, and you couldn't

---

excitement [ɪkˈsaɪtmənt], there's always a lot of excitement before a big football match

to sleep rough [ˈsliːp ˈrʌf], to sleep outside, without a bed

fuss [fʌs], it's only a little cut, don't make such a fuss!

attention [əˈtenʃən], when everyone listens to what you are saying, you have their attention

have it any more."

The doctor smiled.

"It's quite natural to feel like that - but most children *get over* it in a while."

5 "Where can we get the parents' phone number?" Gaynor asked.

"It was in the paper, but I've thrown it out. I'll ring the police station." The doctor pulled a mobile out of her bag.

10 The police didn't just give the doctor the phone number. They came themselves.

Chapter Seven - Time to go home?

A policeman and a policewoman arrived in less than half an hour. They had a photo of Anna with them.

"It's her all right," the man said, in Danish, of course.
15 "I'll tell the parents. We *weren't quite sure* till we saw her. They know a runaway girl has been found. We rang them as soon as the doctor here called us."

"No, please!" Anna said. "I don't want to go back home."

20 "But you can't stay here," the policewoman said.

"She's ill," the doctor said. "Don't be too *hard* on her."

"And why is she ill?" the policeman asked - and answered the question himself. "Because she's living
25 rough and the good weather is over. It's time for her to

to get over something, when you feel better after being ill, you have got over it
to be (quite) sure, to know that something is right or true
hard [hɑːd], (here) unkind, unfriendly

38

go home." He pulled a piece of paper out of his pocket. "This is the number." He went into the kitchen. After a few seconds they heard him talking on his mobile.

Anna began to cry again.

Gaynor put her hand on Anna's arm.   5

"Why don't you want to go home?" she asked.

Well, you know the reasons, and a few minutes later Gaynor, Jane and Michael knew them too. And so did the policewoman.

"I can understand how you feel," the policewoman   10
said. "But we still have to tell your parents where you are. You can see that, can't you."

Anna said nothing.

The policeman came back into the living room.

"Your parents are on their way," he said. "They'll be   15
here in less than an hour. Your father ..."

"He's not my father!" Anna shouted.

"Your stepfather was at work, of course, but he has taken the day off."

39

The police said goodbye and went out to their car. Their job was done.

Anna finished her tea, then she lay down on the sofa and began to cry again quietly. It was not long before another car came slowly down the sandy road and stopped outside. Gaynor went out to meet Anna's parents,

"Hello," she said. "I'm Gaynor Owen. You must be feeling very happy."

"Well," Anna's mother said. "We're happy that Anna is alive and well. You know, when a child is missing for more than a day or two .... But we're still very worried because she ran away from home. We know she still misses her father - it's only natural. But we've tried so hard to help her, haven't we, Lars. Oh, by the way, this is Lars, and I'm Kirsten."

Anna's stepfather nodded. He was a big man who didn't say very much.

"The baby is the problem," he said. He opened the back door of the car. The baby was sleeping in its special seat. Next to it was an empty place - Anna's.

"I must see Anna," her mother said. "How is she - the police said she was ill."

"She's got flu," Gaynor said. "It's not too serious. But another night or two outside, and it could have been very serious. She *dragged* herself to our verandah steps this morning - she was very *weak*."

Anna's mother ran into the house.

"Where is she?" she shouted.

to drag [dræg], (here) to pull yourself along on the ground
weak [wi:k], opposite of strong

40

The sofa in the living room was empty. And the Owen children were nowhere to be seen.

Gaynor ran into the house. She couldn't believe her eyes.

"Jane? Michael?" she called. There was no answer. 5

"They can't be far away." she said. "I'll look in the house. You have a look around outside."

Ten minutes later the three *adults* met on the verandah, without any of the children.

"We can't call the police again," Gaynor said. "We'd 10 look so silly!"

"But what else can we do? Anna is ill. It's *dangerous* for her to be out there."

"Did you look on the beach?" Gaynor asked.

"Yes, we did," replied the stepfather. "But you can't 15 hide down there - there's just sand and someone's inflatable."

"Come on!" Gaynor said. "That's where they are. They must be. We've looked everywhere else."

The boat was turned over to keep the inside dry. 20

Gaynor lifted one end. Inside were three cold and sandy children.

"Thank God!" she said. "Come back to the house, all of you. We've got some serious talking to do."

Anna tried to get up, but she couldn't. 25

Her stepfather picked her up as if she weighed nothing. She *struggled* for a moment and then she lay still. Everyone went slowly back up the path and into the house.

adults ['ædʌlt], people who are not children any more
dangerous, (here) not safe
to struggle ['strʌgl], to try and get away from someone who is holding you

41

They all sat down in the living room. Anna was back on the sofa with a blanket over her.

"Well," Gaynor said to her children. "What have you got to say for yourselves?"

"She doesn't want to go back home," Michael said. "We were just trying to help."

"And you thought that was a good way to help! You should be *ashamed* of yourselves."

"Sorry, Mum," Jane said.

"You should say sorry to Anna's parents!"

"That's all right," Anna's mother said. "The question is, what do we do now? Of course we want to take Anna home with us, but ...."

"Well, she's not too ill to travel," Gaynor said.

Jane's face went very red.

"You can't drag her into your car if she doesn't want to go," she said.

---

to be ashamed of yourself [ə'ʃeimd], to feel bad about something you have done

42

Anna's stepfather smiled.

"Well," he said. "She can't put up much of a *fight*, can she."

"Is that what you're going to do?" Jane said.

"No," the stepfather said. "That can't be the right 5 way."

No one said anything for a while.

Outside in the car the baby began to cry. Anna's mother went out to it.

"Look," Gaynor said. "We've got another week of 10 holiday here. Let Anna stay with us until we go back to Wales. We'll talk to her. I'm sure she knows home is the best place for her. She just needs a bit more time."

"Well, I don't know ..." the stepfather said. "I'll see what Kirsten says." He went out to the car. He and his 15 wife talked quietly to one another for a few minutes.

Then they came back in. Anna's mother was carrying the baby.

"Oh, it's sweet!" Jane said.

"No it isn't, it's horrible!" Anna said. 20

"That decides it," Anna's mother said. "You can stay here with the Owens for now. We'll come and get you next weekend. I suppose you've forgotten all about school and holidays and things like that, Anna. Well, it's the holidays now! You're not missing school any 25 more. We'll telephone every day - we really miss you at home. It's going to be a long week, isn't it Lars."

Anna's stepfather nodded. "Yes," he said. "A long week for us - but a fun week for Anna, I hope."

---

to fight [faɪt], there's a big fight tonight - 'Killer' Jones against 'Hammer' Jenkins

Chapter Eight - Happy families?

Anna soon began to get better, but she wasn't happy. The Owens tried to *cheer her up*, but it was a *hard* job. She just didn't want to play second fiddle to the new baby. Her parents rang her every day, and they both had long talks with her. Was it doing any good? It was hard to say.

Jane and Anna were both sleeping *in bunks* in Jane's room. Before Anna came to stay, Jane was in the top bunk, but she gave Anna the top bunk because she wanted to be nice to her.

Wednesday was a lovely day, but the girls were in no hurry to get up. Suddenly Michael ran into the room like a little *hurricane*, and pulled the duvet off his sister.

"Come on, come on!" he yelled. "The sun's shining and the water's warm. Let's go for a swim before breakfast."

"Go away Michael!" his sister said. "It's *rude* to go into a lady's bedroom without *knocking*."

"Huh!" Michael said. "I don't see any ladies - just two silly girls - *lazy* girls, too."

"And who has been last out of bed every other morning?" Jane asked.

"Er - I don't remember," Michael said.

"Well, I remember - and it was you, of course. And

---

to cheer someone up [tʃɪə], to help someone to feel happy
hard [hɑ:d], (here) not easy
bunks [bʌŋks], one bed above another
hurricane ['hʌrɪkən], a very strong wind
rude [ru:d], don't put your tongue out - it's rude!
to knock [nɒk], a knock is louder than a tap
lazy ['leɪzɪ], someone who doesn't like work is lazy

who nearly always 'forgets' when it's his turn to do something in the kitchen?"

"I - er - forget," Michael said.

"You again," Jane said.

Anna was laughing - for the first time in a very long time. ⁵

"This is great!" she said. "Please go on. I think Jane is winning, Michael. Can't you think of anything your sister does wrong?"

"Well," Michael said. "She's really hopeless with the ¹⁰ computer. When she's trying to do her homework she keeps pressing the wrong button, losing half her text, getting *bullets* where she doesn't want them - and then it's 'Michael, can you come and help me.' It really *gets on my nerves* sometimes." ¹⁵

"What do you say to that, Jane?" Anna asked.

"It's true, I'm afraid. I know it's a *cliché* - that girls are no good with computers - but I really **am** hopeless. Maybe I should play games on the thing, but Michael's games are nearly all *violent*." ²⁰

"Look," Michael said. "This could go on all morning. Are you coming for a swim or not?"

"Yes," Jane said. "Be with you in a couple of minutes."

"I'll come down with you," Anna said, "but I can't go ²⁵ in the water. The doctor said I mustn't go swimming for a week or so."

The two girls walked down to the water together.

bullet ['bʊlɪt], (here) a sign like this: •
it gets on my nerves ['nɔːvz], it makes me angry
cliché ['kliːʃeɪ], something everyone says - but it may not be true
violent ['vaɪələnt], with a lot of fighting etc.

45

"You know," Anna said, "that was really fun for me just now."

"How do you mean? "

"Well, it's nice to have a brother to talk to, don't
5 you think?"

"I'm not so sure. We fight most of the time - Michael really gets on **my** nerves sometimes."

"But you'd miss him if he wasn't there."

"Yes, of course I would."

10 Now the girls were down by the water. Michael was already splashing around, trying to look like a *shark*, or a *submarine* or something.

Jane laughed,

"He's really a lot of fun most of the time - but please
15 don't tell him I said so!"

Anna was looking very *thoughtful*.

"Maybe I could *get used to* my new brother sooner or later - but you can't have much fun with a baby - you just put stuff in one end and it comes out the other!"

20 "Oh Anna!" Jane said. "You're terrible, you really are!"

Michael raced up the beach and splashed the girls. They both screamed, of course.

"What's all this talking?" he said. "Come on Jane,
25 we'll be late for breakfast if you don't hurry up."

Anna sat on the inflatable and watched brother and sister swimming, playing with an old beachball, calling to one another, laughing.

shark

submarine, see vignette, page 48
thoughtful ['θɔːtfəl], thinking quietly about something
to get used to [juːst], to (begin to) feel better/happier about something
or someone

"Yes," she thought. "It's nice to have a brother - but how many years do you have to wait before you can play together?"

The three children walked back to the cottage together. Gaynor watched them from the verandah window.   5

"Anna seems much happier now," she thought, "but there's still something not quite right. I *wonder* what it is."

After breakfast she asked Jane and Michael to wash up. For once they didn't *complain*.   10

She took Anna out onto the verandah with her. They sat down together.

"You're feeling better about things, aren't you Anna," Gaynor said.

"Yes - it's great to see Jane and Michael together. We   15 could be like that one day, but ..."

"But ... ?"

"Well, it will be years before I can play with our baby."

Gaynor smiled.   20

"You don't know how wrong you are!"

"How do you mean?"

"Well, a baby learns so much in its first couple of years - more than in the rest of its life - seeing things clearly, walking, talking - and it's really wonderful to   25 watch all this happening."

"For the mother, maybe."

"But it could be wonderful for you, too - babies need to play a lot. That's how they learn. And you can soon

---

to wonder ['wʌndə], (here) to try and find an answer to a problem
to complain [kəm'pleɪn], to say you don't like something

47

have a lot of fun with them. Have you ever put your *cheek* against the baby's cheek?"

"No. Why would I want to?"

"It's so soft - and babies have a nice smell, too."

5   "Not when they need a new *nappy*!"

"No! You're right there - but changing nappies is *part of the package*. The fun and the work go together. You could be a big help to your mother - and stepfather - if you wanted to."

10   Anna looked thoughtfully down towards the fjord.

"I wonder," Gaynor thought. "Does she think I'm trying to *brainwash* her - or is she beginning to see things differently?"

submarine

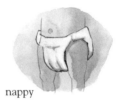
nappy

Anna didn't run out to meet her parents when they 15   came to take her home. She waited in the cottage. She was feeling a bit worried, and somehow a bit *shy*. But she knew what she had to do.

Gaynor and the children came back into the cottage with Anna's family, all talking rather loudly. Then they 20   saw Anna, and the talking stopped.

Anna went to her mother.

part of the package ['pækɪdʒ], you have to take the nice and the not so nice parts together
to brainwash ['breɪnwɒʃ], to tell someone something again and again until they believe it
shy [ʃaɪ], a bit afraid of other people

48

cheek

"Can I hold the baby?" she asked.

Her mother was surprised.

"Yes, of course. Here you are."

Anna took the baby, and carefully put her hand under its little head. She lifted the baby until she could put its soft cheek against hers. 5

"Well, Anna," her mother said. "This is a surprise - we're so pleased - I can't tell you - we were so worried - but now ... "

Anna held the baby away from her. 10

"Yuk!" she said. "He needs a new nappy - and if you think I'm going to change it ..."

Her mother smiled.

"Don't worry. I'll do it."

"I'll come with you. I want to see how it's done." 15

Mother and daughter disappeared into the bathroom.

Lars and Gaynor looked at one another.

"I don't know what you did," Lars said, "but thank

you. I've brought some little presents for Anna, but she doesn't need them now."

"Yes, she does. You have to show her that she's important, too. She hates playing second fiddle to the baby - but she's going to play **with** it from now on - that's quite a big step in the right direction."

Kirsten and Anna came back with the baby - smelling nice now. After drinks and biscuits, and a bottle for the baby, after the thank yous and goodbyes, Anna's family went down to their car. A visit to Wales was promised for the next summer.

Everyone waved. The car bumped along the track to the main road. Then it was gone.

"Well," Gaynor said. "I think Anna learnt quite a lot from you two."

"But I'm sure she learnt more from you, Mum," Jane said. They went back into the cottage. Suddenly it seemed very empty and quiet.

"Anna is really so lucky," Jane said. "She's got a new brother *and* a new dad."

"Will we have a new Dad one day?" Michael asked.

"I don't know," Gaynor said. "We're a pretty good team as we are, don't you think? Let's have a last picnic down on the beach, then it will be time to start packing."

Questions and activities

Chapter One
1. Can you remember the names of the Owen family. And what about Mr. Owen?
2. Where are the Owens spending their holiday this year?
3. Where's the key?
4. What's nice about the girl's room? And the boy's room?
5. What's in the coolbox before they go down to the water ... and what's in it when Michael looks in the box?

Chapter Two
a) Feeling uneasy
What makes you feel uneasy, or a bit worried or frightened? Here are some ideas:
- Dark nights.
- Big dogs.
- Going into a cellar (a dark room under a house).
- Going very fast in a car.
- Flying.
- Detective films on TV.

Ask your friends. Like this:
- Are you afraid of big dogs?
  No, I like big dogs!
- How about flying?
  Well, I'm a bit worried, but flying is OK.

How about you?
- I don't like .... but I'm not frightened of ...
- ...

b) What happened in this chapter?

Can you put the pieces in the right order?

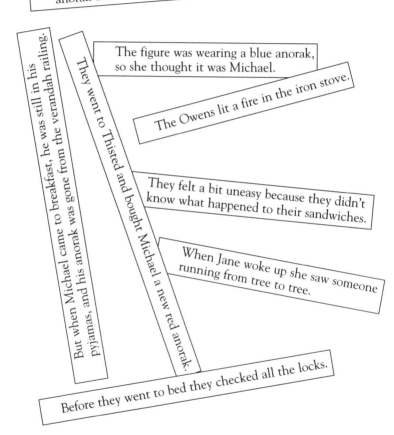

When they got back, someone had put his old blue anorak back on the railing.

The figure was wearing a blue anorak, so she thought it was Michael.

The Owens lit a fire in the iron stove.

They felt a bit uneasy because they didn't know what happened to their sandwiches.

When Jane woke up she saw someone running from tree to tree.

But when Michael came to breakfast, he was still in his pyjamas, and his anorak was gone from the verandah railing.

They went to Thisted and bought Michael a new red anorak.

Before they went to bed they checked all the locks.

Chapter Three
a) The trap
Try to fill in the missing words.
They put a _____ on the verandah _____, then moved the table to the _____ of the verandah, near the _____. Then they fixed a piece of _____ to the cake. They fixed the other end to a _____ _____. If someone took the cake, the _____ _____ would fall off the table, and there would be a big _____!

b) The thief ...
... borrowed the anorak because ...
... took food because ...
... couldn't get to a shop because ... so he or she ...
... would be uneasy in a shop because ...

c) You understand, don't you!
The doctor needs her car if she gets an _____. But it won't _____ because there's no _____ in the _____ _____.
The petrol from the doctor's car ended up in _____.
So if Michael gives her some of the petrol for the out-board, he's really giving back _____.

Chapter Four
Anna's problems
The diagram below shows Anna's problems. How much can you remember about them? Try to write a sentence or two for each problem.

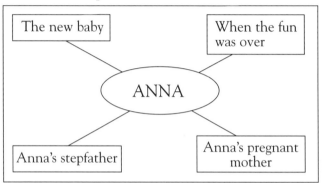

Chapter Five
Some why-questions
1. Why is Anna late?
2. Why are the police too busy to look for her?
3. Why is Anna hungry?
4. Why can't she go back to 'her' shed?
5. Why can't she get back to sleep the second night?

Chapter Six
If you're ill ...
Most people get a _____
now and then.

It can get worse, then we talk about having _____
Sometimes people even get something much worse. It's called _____.

If you're ill, you have to see a _____.
He or she will _____ you.
Then you usually get a _____,
which you take to the _____.
It could be for some _____.
And you'll soon be well again!

Chapter Seven
Useful expressions

There are a lot of expressions which don't always mean very much on their own, but they can make your English much more natural. Find the right ones below - they're all in chapter 7. Try to learn them - then test yourself and your neighbour.

For example: The policeman doesn't just say "It's her." He says, "It's her **all right**."
Now try these:

• Jane and Michael knew them too. And ____ _____ the policewoman.
• You can see that, _____ _____.
• Your parents are _____ _____ _____.
• He has taken _____ _____ _____.
  _____, we're happy that Anna is alive and well.
• ___ ____, when a child is missing for a day or two ...
• Oh, ___ ____ ___. this is Lars, and I'm Kirsten.
• But ___ _____ can we do?
• We've looked _____ _____.
• "_____ _____ _____," Anna's mother said.
• ___ _____ we want to take Anna home with us, but ...
• ____ ____ she knows home is the best place for her.
• You can stay here with the Owens ____ ____.

Chapter Eight

a) Thoughts and feelings

1. Why was Anna still not happy?
2. Who usually gets up late?
3. What problems does Jane have with her computer?
4. Why does Anna say, "That was really fun for me just now"?
5. Why does Jane say, "You're terrible, you really are!"?
6. What does Gaynor tell Anna about babies?
7. Is Lars right when he say Anna doesn't need little presents? If not, why not?
8. How do the Owens feel after Anna and her family have gone?

b) *Your* thoughts

1. Do you think Anna will be happy at home now?
2. Do you like babies? Give your reasons.
3. If you have any brothers or sisters, say how you get on with them. If you don't, you can talk about your best friend.
4. Would you like a holiday in a holiday cottage? Give your reasons, and talk about other kinds of holiday, too - a camping or caravanning holiday, a holiday on a farm with ponies etc., a hotel on Majorca, skiing, back-packing, safari ... Try to say what you would like or not like. What plans has your family made for next summer?
5. What did you think of the story? Try to write a few lines about it, saying which parts you liked or didn't like.
6. Re-tell your favourite part of the story in your own words. Don't copy it from the book!